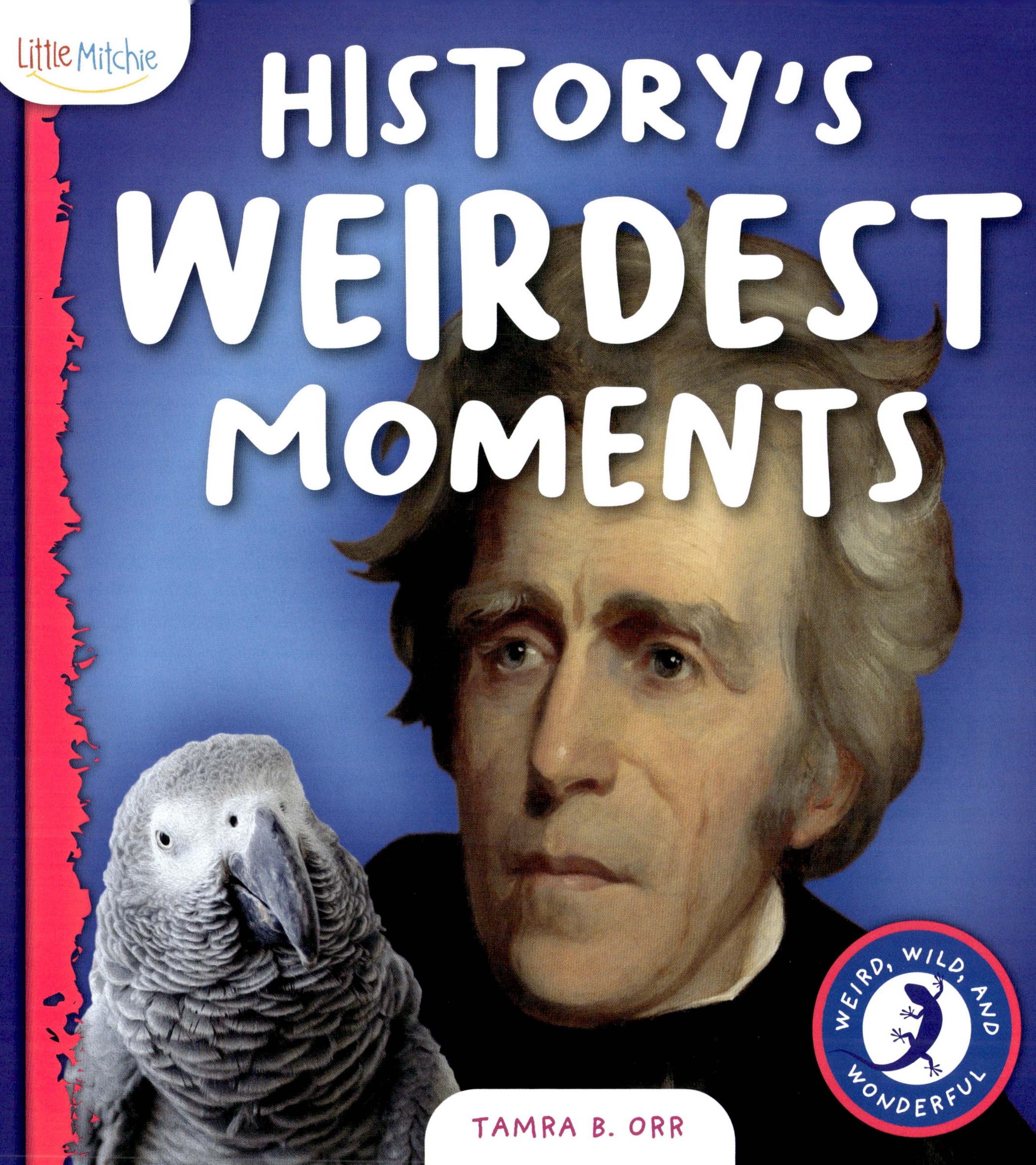
Little Mitchie
HISTORY'S WEIRDEST MOMENTS
WEIRD, WILD, AND WONDERFUL
TAMRA B. ORR

CREATING YOUNG NONFICTION READERS

Little Mitchie books spark curiosity and support early nonfiction reading for students in Grades 2-3. Designed to build vocabulary, support second language learners, and prepare readers for middle-grade content, each book includes helpful tips for parents and educators to build confidence and deepen understanding of the world.

TIPS FOR READING NONFICTION WITH BEGINNING READERS

Talk about Nonfiction

Begin by explaining that nonfiction books give us information that is true. The book will be organized around a specific topic or idea, and we may learn new facts through reading.

Look at the Parts

Most nonfiction books have helpful features. Our *Little Mitchie* titles include color photographs and graphic aids, a table of contents, a glossary, and an index. Share the purpose of these features with your reader.

Color Photos and Graphic Aids

A lot of information can be found by "reading" photos, charts, maps, and other graphic aids found within nonfiction texts. Help your reader learn more about the different ways information can be displayed.

Table of Contents

Located at the front of the book, this list shows the big ideas within the text and the page numbers where they can be found.

Glossary

Located at the back of the book, the glossary defines key words and phrases that are related to the topic. These words and phrases can be found in the text in colored type.

Index

Located at the back of the book, an index is an alphabetical list of topics and the page numbers where they can be found.

With a little help and guidance about reading nonfiction, you can feel good about introducing a young reader to the world of *Little Mitchie* nonfiction books.

Little Mitchie is an imprint of:

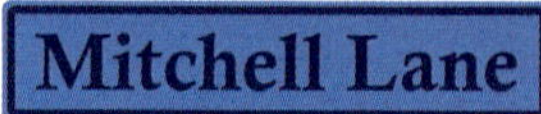

PUBLISHERS

2001 SW 31st Avenue
Hallandale, FL 33009
mitchelllanepub.com

First Edition, 2027.

Author: Tamra B. Orr
Designer: Jen Bowers
Editor: Tricia Hoffman
Library of Congress Cataloging-in-Publication Data
Title: History's Weirdest Moments / by Tamra Orr

Description: Hallandale, FL :
Mitchell Lane Publishers, [2027]

Identifiers:
ISBN 979-8-89260-893-0 (library bound)
ISBN 979-8-89260-996-8 (eBook)

Library of Congress Control Number: 2026936370

PHOTO CREDITS
Shutterstock: cover, p.1 ©2016 Everett Collection, cover, p.1, p.11 ©2018 Natalia Johnson (paint filter applied), p.5 ©2016 Ysbrand Cosijn, p.6 ©2024 ShahidPhotogharapher, p.7 ©2025 Nigel J. Harris, Public Domain 1942 collections of the Imperial War Museums, p.8 ©2025 Shutterstock AI, p.9 ©2020 Nicoleta Ionescu, p.10–11 ©2023 Jakub Maculewicz, p.13 ©2017 Darryl Brooks, Public Domain 1959, p.14 ©2015 Everett Collection, p.15 ©2025 Rawpixel.com, ©2015 Everett Collection, p.16–17 ©2018 Golden House Images, p.18 ©2018 iPreech Studio, p.19 ©2023 puha dorin, p.20 ©2024 Shutterstock AI, p.21 ©2021 Angata, p.22 ©2014 Anaite, ©2021 Sergii Chernov ©2016 Andrea Izzotti

TABLE OF CONTENTS

Chapter One

DID THAT REALLY HAPPEN?

History is full of fascinating leaders, terrible tragedies, and incredible victories. But it is also full of truly weird moments. They are the kind where you read and wonder, did that really happen? Yes, it did!

FASHION CRIME ALERT

In 1922, men wore straw hats, but only between May 15 and September 15. If caught wearing one before or after that, it was taken and destroyed! That led to **riots** in several cities.

Chapter Two

CRAZY CRITTERS

In 1932 Australia, soldiers were tasked with getting rid of emus that were ruining crops. They thought it would be easy. Wrong! The emus were too fast. In the end, the birds "won" the Great Emu War.

A POLISH SOLDIER

In 1943, the Polish Corps had a new **recruit**—a brown bear named Wojtek. He was a favorite with the soldiers. He helped carry equipment during battle and played games during quiet times. He held the **rank** of Private and was later promoted!

Imagine military leader Napoleon Bonaparte defeated by ... rabbits? A hunt turned into a disaster! Instead of running away, the rabbits swarmed Napoleon. Why? They were tame rabbits, not wild, and expected to be fed.

Put 'em up! During the 1920s, some of the most popular boxers were kangaroos! Like humans, they could punch. They often won! But animal rights groups put a stop to the fights to protect the **marsupials**.

A SALTY PARROT

In 1845, former president Andrew Jackson died. At his funeral, one guest swore so loudly and so often that it had to be taken out. It was Jackson's pet African parrot, Poll.

Chapter Three

PECULIAR PEOPLE

Have you ever noticed laughter is **contagious**? In 1962 Tanzania, one girl began laughing and couldn't stop! The laughter kept spreading. Months later, almost 1,000 people were laughing. More than a dozen schools closed!

JUST ONE MORE!

In the late 1950s, colleges around the world began trying to set a new record for how many people could be stuffed into a phone booth! The winners came from South Africa. They got 25 people squashed tightly inside.

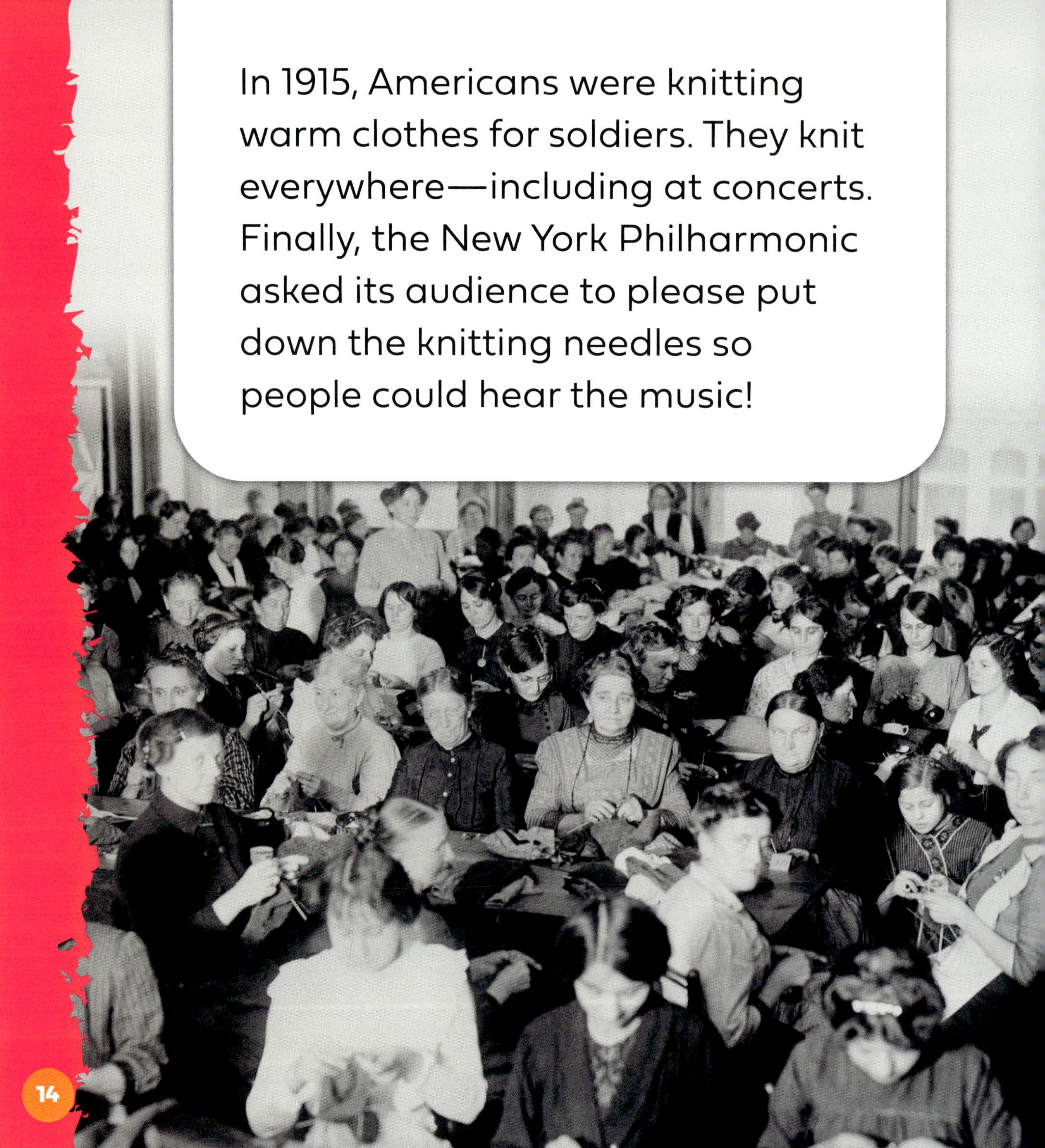

In 1915, Americans were knitting warm clothes for soldiers. They knit everywhere—including at concerts. Finally, the New York Philharmonic asked its audience to please put down the knitting needles so people could hear the music!

THE ALEXANDRA LIMP

When Alexandra, Princess of Wales, fell ill, it left her with a limp. Wealthy women so admired her that they began limping to imitate her. Shoe stores even began selling pairs of shoes with different heels to make it easier!

In 1879, 13 men entered a new kind of race: pedestrianism, or competitive walking. Racers walked around a track in New York City for six days straight. They needed to walk at least 450 miles (724 km)!

Chapter Four

EXTRA ODDNESS

Floods happen sometimes. But the Boston flood in 1919 was different. A huge tank full of molasses burst. More than two million gallons (76 billion L) of the sticky stuff crushed buildings and homes.

PLEASE FLY AWAY

Pepi II, an Egyptian pharaoh around 2200 BC, disliked flies. So, he had his servants cover themselves in honey. That way, the insects would land on them instead of him!

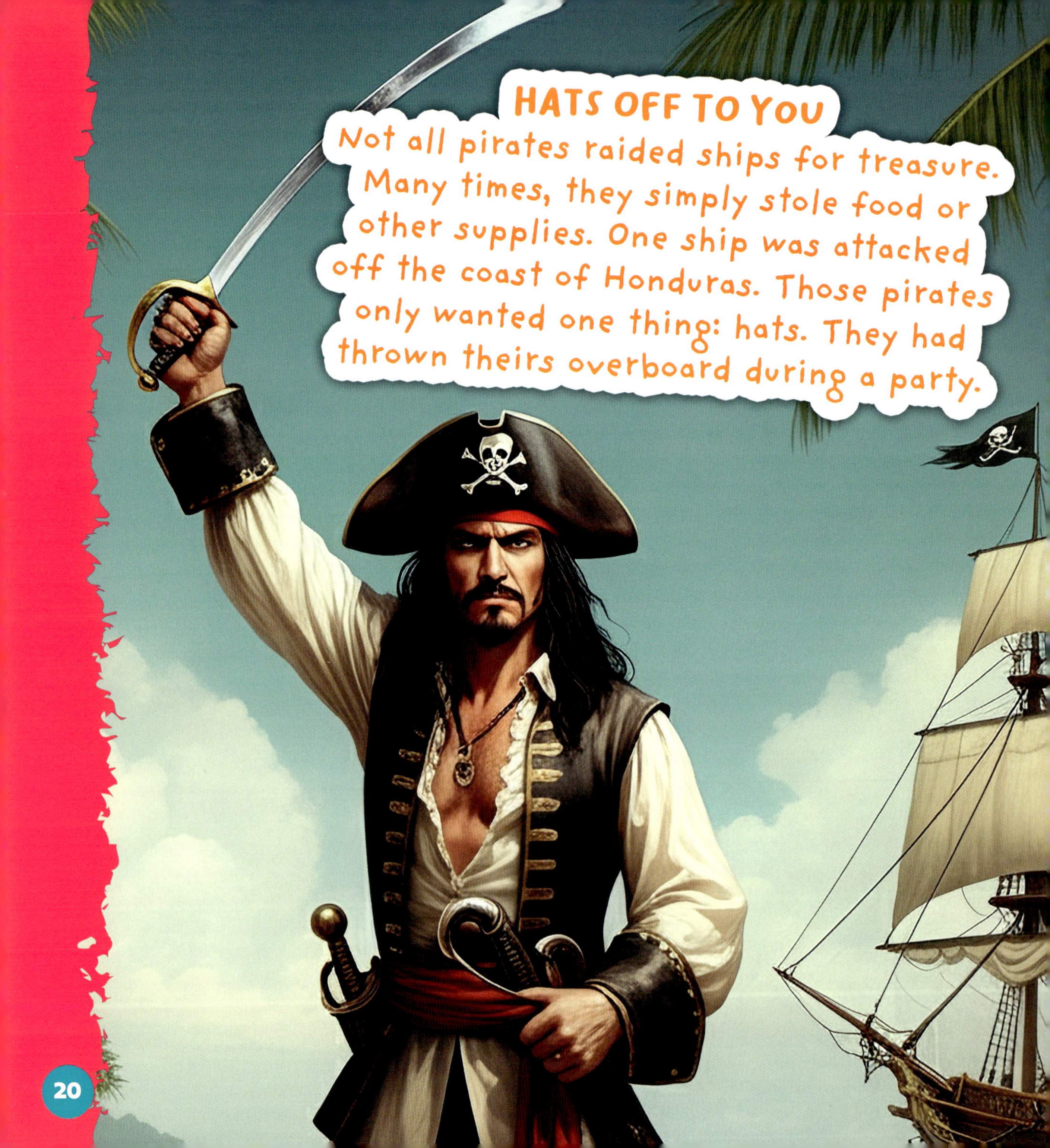

HATS OFF TO YOU

Not all pirates raided ships for treasure. Many times, they simply stole food or other supplies. One ship was attacked off the coast of Honduras. Those pirates only wanted one thing: hats. They had thrown theirs overboard during a party.

Pilots use many **navigation** tools. But for almost a century, some have used Hector the **Convector**. It is a thundercloud that appears off Australia's northern coast every day from September through March at 3 p.m. Follow that cloud!

EVEN WILDER!

In the early 20th century, people loved to watch horse diving. Horses would jump into pools from diving boards up to 60 feet (18 m) high!

In California, they used to have alligator farms. Visitors could eat and rest right next to trained gators!

In the mid-19th century, Egyptian street vendors often sold mummies as **souvenirs**.

GLOSSARY

contagious (kuhn-tay-juhs) carrying or spreading a disease

convector (kuhn-vek-ter) a rising column of warm, moist air

marsupial (mahr-soo-pee-uhl) a mammal that has a pouch

navigation (nav-i-gay-shuhn) directing the course of a ship or aircraft

rank (rangk) a position in the armed forces

recruit (ri-kroot) someone who has recently joined a group or military

riots (rye-uhtz) noisy, violent public disturbances caused by a group of people

souvenirs (soo-vuh-neerz) objects that you keep to remind you of a place

FURTHER READING

Graham, Matthew, and Rebecca Whitlock. *Absolutely Absurd History.* Willow & Bloom Publishing, 2025.

Ward, Michelle. *The Big Book of Fun Facts for Young Kids.* Harbor & Ink Press, 2025.

ON THE INTERNET

Weird But True!: History
https://kids.nationalgeographic.com/weird-but-true/article/history
National Geographic presents videos, articles, and more about very strange but true history.

50 Best Fun History Facts for Kids
https://www.beano.com/facts/school/history-facts
Take a look at some more of the wildest events in history!

INDEX